Class 33

MARK V. PIKE

Title page image: Preserved 'Slim Jim' 33201 is seen stabled in the bay platform at Swanage station. 28 December 2015.

Contents page image: Preserved twins D6575 (33057) and D6566 (33048) are seen coupled together at Blue Anchor station on the West Somerset Railway whilst working a Minehead to Bishops Lydeard service. 10 June 2018.

Rear cover image: West Coast Railway Company (WCRC) 33025 *Glen Falloch* is seen in the sidings at Weymouth after working in with a charter train. 23 August 2008.

Published by Key Books
An imprint of Key Publishing Ltd
PO Box 100
Stamford
Lincs PE9 1XQ

www.keypublishing.com

The right of Mark V. Pike to be identified as the author of this book has been asserted in accordance with the Copyright, Designs and Patents Act 1988 Sections 77 and 78.

Typeset by SJmagic DESIGN SERVICES, India.

Contents

Introduction

Introduced in 1960, a class of 98 locomotives, later to be designated as Class 33s, were built by the Birmingham Railway Carriage and Wagon Company, capable of operating up to 85mph and equipped with a reliable 1,550hp Sulzer engine. Most of the class were built to a standard width of 9ft 3in, but the last 12 examples were just 8ft 8in wide to enable them to operate through the narrow tunnels on the Hastings line, earning them the nickname of 'Slim Jims'.

In 1967, 19 locos were selected for conversion to work in push-pull mode (and were subsequently nicknamed 'bagpipes') for use as part of the Waterloo to Bournemouth third rail electrification scheme, so that they could operate with the new 4-TC trailer units beyond Bournemouth to Weymouth, which remained un-electrified until 1988. In total, three sub-classes were created, classified as standard Class 33/0, push-pull Class 33/1 and narrow-bodied Class 33/2.

The locos eventually spread their wings far and wide to a large area of operation, and throughout their careers worked both passenger and freight duties alike. However, it was always the Southern Region that saw the main bulk of their workings, with allocations split between Hither Green, Stewarts Lane and Eastleigh.

In addition to the Bournemouth to Weymouth push-pull diagrams, the locos could also be found working West of England services from Waterloo to Salisbury and Exeter St Davids, especially after the early 1970s when the Class 42 'Warship' diesel hydraulics had been withdrawn. They also worked alongside the Class 50s on these services until the present Class 159 units were introduced in 1993. Portsmouth Harbour to Reading, Clapham Junction to Kensington Olympia, and numerous freight services across the south and beyond were all regularly worked by them as well.

During the 1980s, they were also diagrammed on passenger services much further afield, such as Portsmouth Harbour to Bristol/Cardiff/Swansea, Cardiff to Crewe/Manchester, Crewe to Holyhead, and even local services from Exeter to Barnstaple/Paignton/Plymouth.

Following privatisation, freight company English Welsh & Scottish Railway (EWS) even transferred three members of the class to Aberdeen, albeit not for very long. All this amounted to a very useful class of locos, and many survive into the 21st century on heritage lines and charter services.

Chapter 1

Main Lines 1985–2000

The first section of the book concentrates on Class 33s during their latter days of British Rail (BR) operation on a variety of different trains, mostly in their usual area of operation in the south of England.

Templecombe station in Somerset is very much a shadow of its former self these days, the wide expanse of trees and bushes behind the signal box and to the rear of the train were once occupied by a large and busy marshalling yard. The only surviving items from its heyday are the platforms themselves and the signal box, as well as the goods shed on the left. It was the junction for the famous Somerset & Dorset Railway, whose line used to enter the station to the right of the signal box via a bay platform. This whole area, apart from the signal box, was closed in the late 1960s when the line was decimated. However, after years of campaigning, the station reopened during 1983, and during the late 2010s, a new platform face was constructed to the left of this picture, effectively making the platform to the right redundant. 33102 is entering with 4-TC unit 8001 as the 11.55 Exeter St Davids to London Waterloo, which was an unusual use of loco and stock, probably arranged at the last minute due to stock shortages. This loco has since moved into preservation and can be found on the Churnet Valley Railway. 21 May 1991.

From a different viewpoint, we see 33035 approaching Templecombe with another Exeter St Davids to London Waterloo service. As can be seen from the pointwork under the train, the line reverts to double track from here as far as Yeovil Junction. This is another loco that has since entered preservation, currently earning its keep on the Ecclesbourne Valley Railway. 11 October 1986.

The last image from Templecombe as we see 33119, deputising for a Class 50, approaching with an Exeter St Davids to London Waterloo service. I have no idea what the gentleman by the grey lineside cabinet was up to, but he was clearly trespassing. It all seemed much less of an issue back then! This loco was scrapped in April 1992. 6 June 1987.

Spitfire

We now move to Salisbury, where we see 33047 *Spitfire* having just arrived with a terminating service from London Waterloo, while pulling in alongside is 47710 with a Waterloo to Exeter St Davids service. This Class 33 lasted until February 1997, when it was finally disposed of, and the name was then transferred to 33035, while 47710 was scrapped in 2007. 18 June 1991.

33102 is seen again as it arrives at Salisbury with 2V13, the 12.40 Waterloo to Exeter St Davids, which it worked throughout. As can be observed in this shot, in the early 1990s this loco had an extra front pipe fitted below its central headlight for trial operation with rail head cleaning equipment; no other locos received this addition. 28 June 1992.

This is 33051 awaiting departure from Salisbury with a Portsmouth Harbour to Cardiff Central service. At this time, these cross-country services were regular diagrams for the locos and were usually formed of four or five Mk.1 coaches. Despite this loco being removed from service during August 1998, it was not disposed of until October 2003. 10 April 1987.

Westbury is the location for the next five images, all of which were taken on the same day. First up is 33027 *Earl Mountbatten of Burma*, approaching with 1O36, the 10.10 Cardiff Central to Portsmouth Harbour service, which it had worked from Bristol Temple Meads. Withdrawn from service in 1991, this loco was disposed of around a year or so later, with its nameplates being transferred to 33207. 21 December 1987.

Next, we see 33020 departing with 1V54, the 10.10 Portsmouth Harbour to Swansea service, which it will have worked to Bristol Temple Meads only, where a fresh loco would continue the journey. This loco was withdrawn during 1993 and disposed of four years later during 1997. 21 December 1987.

This is 'celebrity' BR green-liveried 33008 *Eastleigh* departing with 1V46, the 08.30 Brighton to Cardiff Central, which again it worked as far as Bristol Temple Meads. It was painted by Eastleigh Depot into green livery during 1986 and retained it, in two spells, until withdrawal in early 1997, so it was almost a foregone conclusion that this loco would be preserved. It is currently on the Battlefield Line undergoing restoration. 21 December 1987.

The last shot at Westbury sees 33026 getting underway with 1V62, the 12.10 Portsmouth Harbour to Cardiff Central, which it will work as far as Bristol Temple Meads again. This loco once again lingered long after withdrawal in 1998, until it was finally disposed of in 2003. 21 December 1987.

After servicing and fuelling at Bristol Bath Road depot, later in the day 33008 *Eastleigh* is seen arriving back with 1O43, the 14.00 Cardiff Central to Portsmouth Harbour service. 21 December 1987.

A very clean-looking 33004 is at Bristol Temple Meads, having has just come off its train from Portsmouth Harbour. Compared to some examples, this loco was scrapped pretty quickly, withdrawn during 1991 and disposed of in 1992. Circa 1987.

33052 *Ashford* was one of the early recipients of a name in the early 1980s. The loco is seen between duties stabled at the once-busy Bristol Bath Road Depot, now but a memory. Happily, the loco is not just a memory and can currently be found on the Bluebell Railway in Sussex undergoing restoration. Circa 1987.

Ticking over after arrival at Bristol Temple Meads, 33013 is about to be removed from a Portsmouth Harbour to Cardiff Central service. This was another of the early withdrawals during 1989, being reduced to scrap during 1991. Circa 1985.

The highest numbered and last of the class to be built, 'Slim Jim' 33212 is seen at Newport with 1V54, the 10.10 Portsmouth Harbour to Swansea service that it had worked from Bristol Temple Meads. This loco was an even earlier withdrawal, just five months after the date of this image actually, and was scrapped in 1991. 'Slim Jim' was the nickname for these former Hastings gauge locos that were noticeably narrower than the standard locos to allow them to work through the restricted tunnels between Tunbridge Wells and Hastings. 10 April 1987.

From the newest loco to one of the oldest, we see 33002 waiting to depart Crewe with the empty stock of an earlier arrival from Cardiff Central. Another fortunate loco, this one can now be found fully operational on the South Devon Railway. 7 August 1985.

Merlin

Reading was always an excellent place to see Class 33 action, mostly on freight services. The driver is on the trackside phone to the signaller as his ballast train, hauled by 33202 *The Burma Star* and 33046 *Merlin*, waits patiently in the old down through line for a clear path amongst the plethora of other services operating to and from here. Both of these locos are still with us in 2022 amazingly enough, although 33202 has fared much better. Dispensed with by EWS during 1998 and then seeing further main line work during the 2000s, it is now based on the Mid Norfolk Railway, whereas 33046 also withdrawn during 1998 now resides at the East Lancashire Railway as a source of spares and is unlikely to run again. 21 July 1992.

This is quite a load for a single Class 33, even though it is empty stock. 33020 passes through the original platform four with a long rake of Mk.1 stock that was destined to be used for an upcoming charter service in the south of England. Circa 1992.

A smart-looking 33047 passes through platform nine with a long rake of ballast wagons forming an unknown working heading west, possibly for either Didcot or Eastleigh. 3 April 1991.

Many of the departmental ballast workings that passed through the station were double-headed, very often by Class 33s. This is 'Dutch'-liveried 33057 *Seagull* and 33202 *The Burma Star.* Both of these locos again are thankfully still with us in 2022, with 33057 based on the West Somerset Railway and 33202 on the Mid Norfolk Railway. 28 January 1992.

Isle of Grain

Seen at the same spot, but this time with no train in, are 33050 *Isle Of Grain* and 33064 both in Railfreight Construction livery heading west, possibly to Eastleigh or Westbury. Since withdrawal from BR service. 33050 was scrapped in early 1997 while 33064 suffered a similar fate later the same year. 21 April 1992.

Another pair in the down through line awaiting to proceed west are 'Dutch'-liveried duo 33118 and 33019 *Griffon*. After becoming redundant from Bournemouth to Weymouth operations after May 1988, the Class 33/1s were incorporated within the general pool of locos for a variety of duties. A couple of differing outcomes befell these two upon withdrawal from service. 33118 was scrapped during 1997, but 33019 entered preservation; however, as far as I am aware, it has not worked under its own power as yet. At the present time, it is stored at Nemesis Rail, Burton upon Trent. 19 February 1992.

A bit of an unusual working here, as 33116 and 47600 have arrived with a westbound parcels train. It was believed that the Class 47 had failed en route and was rescued by the '33', as both locos are in the process of being removed here. Yet again, both locos are still with us today; 33116 is currently out of service on the Great Central Railway, while 47600 (later 47744) is now quietly rusting away in the yard at Nemesis Rail, Burton upon Trent. 14 August 1991.

You could not miss this one! 33021 *Eastleigh* stands at Old Oak Common during an open day. The loco was first painted bright red in the late 1990s after being purchased from BR, apparently by a private couple who had worked for the Post Office, hence the red livery. Later, it went on to operate back on the main line for Fragonset Railways (since disbanded), mainly for hauling new Desiro units on the Southern Region during the early 2000s. It has now re-entered preservation and can be found at the Churnet Valley Railway in operational condition and back in Post Office red livery. 5 August 2000.

Members of the class have often been featured at various depot open days over the years. This is 33203 after withdrawal from service on display at Eastleigh Works open day. The years after BR dispensed with it from 1991 were a sad, drawn out affair. It was initially sold to Harry Needle in October 1992 but never saw use again with any owner, passing from pillar to post until it was finally disposed of in May 2006. 27 September 1992.

As mentioned earlier in this book, the repainting of 33008 *Eastleigh* into BR green livery assured its 'celebrity' status and a place in preservation, and it was also the first of the class to be officially named back in 1980. It is seen here just after its revised (and more historically accurate) green repaint at the Eastleigh Depot open day. Entering private ownership in 1997, it is another loco to have swapped owners over the years and not turned a wheel under its own power. It is currently undergoing restoration on the Battlefield Line, so hopefully it will be up and running in the not-too-distant future. 12 October 1986.

Six years later, and 33008 *Eastleigh* is seen on display again, here in the main carriage shed at the Bournemouth Depot open day attached to a breakdown crane. By this time, the loco had regained its D6508 number it received when new, and there are also a couple more slight revisions to the livery. Incidentally, as I write this in 2022, a newly converted Class 69, 69005, that has been rebuilt and re-engineered from a former Class 56 has recently been released to traffic in a livery very similar to this and named *Eastleigh* as well. 12 September 1992.

During my time working on the railway, I was lucky enough to be able to visit areas that were out of bounds to the general public. One of these was the signal box at Bournemouth Central, situated high above the station canopy, where we see 33105 and 33101 stabled in the old parcels dock awaiting their next duties. Bournemouth signal box was closed back in mid-December 2003 but is still in situ, being a listed building. There have been rumblings over the years that it might form some sort of museum or visitor attraction, but nothing has ever come of this. 33101 was disposed of during 1997, but 33105 was involved in an accident in 1987 and scrapped in 1990. 19 March 1987.

This is 33112 *Templecombe*, also stabled in the old parcel dock at Bournemouth. Note the unofficial addition of the black window surrounds, the only loco that ever appeared like this. Just to the left of this image used to be the loco turntable associated with the steam depot that has long passed into history. Unfortunately, the loco too has passed on, again as the result of an accident in 1988. It was disposed of during 1992 with the nameplates (without the additional plaques) being transferred to Class 47 47315. 17 February 1988.

Although their days on the Bournemouth to Weymouth push-pull services were now over, the Class 33/1s could still be seen semi-regularly in the area after May 1988. This is 33114 *Sultan* and 33102 waiting to depart Bournemouth after taking over from Class 45 45106 with 1Z37, the 06.00 Manchester Piccadilly to Manchester Piccadilly via Eastleigh, Bournemouth and Weymouth 'The Wessex Adventurer' organised by Pathfinder Tours. 33114 received its name, which it only carried for a few months, from the previously withdrawn 33025, while it was scrapped during 1997. 33102, however, can now be found operating on the Churnet Valley Railway, now carrying the name *Sophie*. 5 November 1988.

33114 later lost its *Sultan* nameplates and was re-christened *Ashford 150* at the same time as becoming one of just two of the class to be painted in Network SouthEast (NSE) livery. It also became quite a popular loco, but, despite this, it was withdrawn in 1993 and disposed of in 1997. It is seen here hauling 4-VEP unit 3480, forming a special shuttle service at Bournemouth station heading for the open day being held at Bournemouth Depot that weekend. 12 September 1992.

Above: Another duty that often produced an example of the class in later years was the movement of withdrawn slam-door Southern Region stock to South Wales for scrapping. This is plain grey departmental-liveried 33116 passing through Newport station. This loco is currently operational on the Great Central Railway. 27 February 1992.

Left: A year on from the previous image, and this time we see 33109 passing Salisbury with another rake of condemned units bound for South Wales. This loco is currently operational on the East Lancashire Railway. 23 February 1993.

33208 was one of the earliest privately-owned examples of the class to return to the main line in the late 1990s, mainly for charter use based at the Mid Hants Railway, but it also did a stint in the Welsh Valleys on timetabled passenger services, as well as elsewhere. Here, the '33' had been providing the electric supply behind 'Black Five' 44767 *George Stephenson* on the 1Z33 Waterloo to Poole via Petersfield charter. However, the steam loco was removed here at Southampton Central for servicing at Eastleigh, while 33208 continued on to Poole. As far as I know, this has been the only appearance of this particular 'Black Five' at this location, certainly in the preservation era. 31 January 1998.

Seen earlier at the Old Oak Common open day, 33021 *Eastleigh* was reinstated to traffic as a privately-owned loco during 1997. Wearing its red livery, it was used for a few charter trains prior to going on hire to Fragonset Railways for a while in the early 2000s. It is seen at Paddock Wood top and tailing Bulleid Pacific 34016 *Bodmin* during the first day of the Maidstone Borough Council-organised 'Celebration of Steam and Transport' weekend. 28 August 2000.

In early 1992, there were a series of charter trains run by DC Railtours, mostly starting from London Waterloo, which went to various West Country destinations and proved to be a bit of a money spinner, as they employed a variety of different traction that were often way off their normal operating areas of the time. One such charter was 1Z33, the 09.30 London Waterloo to Paignton, which featured 60029 *Ben Nevis* and 33012 from Waterloo to Salisbury, from where 31201, 31319 and 33101 took over to Exeter St Davids. The strange ensemble is seen awaiting departure from Salisbury. Of these locos, 33101 was detailed earlier in this book, while 31201 was scrapped during 2004 and 31319 succumbed in 2007. Note Class 47/7 47706 approaching in the distance with an Exeter St Davids to London Waterloo service. 29 November 1992.

Another charter train that ran on one of the wettest days I think I have ever experienced! This is 33206 on the Weymouth Quay tramway with 1Z40, the 05.40 Preston to Preston via Weymouth Quay 'Barchester Chronicle' charter organised by A1A Charters. 31145 and 31200 took the train down to the quay and then followed the train back up light engines, before reforming to triple head with the '33' away from Weymouth later. A repeat of this tour is now totally impossible, not least after the lifting of the tramway in the late 2010s. Of these locos, 33206 was scrapped during 1997, while 31145 was reduced to scrap in 1999 and 31200 in 2007. 14 May 1994.

This is 33102 propelling 4-TC units 417 and 410 away from Eastleigh with an unidentified empty stock working in the pouring rain, but this time only a heavy shower! The two 4-TC units were the last ones in service at this time. 29 May 1992.

Another charter to utilise a '33' was 1Z24, the 10.12 Waterloo to Waterloo via Eastleigh Depot Loop and Hamworthy Quay, entitled 'The Hamworthy Quay Phoenix' and again organised by DC Railtours. 33114 is seen arriving at Poole on the return run from Hamworthy Quay, while on the rear at this point were 37227 and 37902. The Class 33's history was outlined earlier in the book, while 37227 was withdrawn during 2004 and is now preserved at the Chinnor and Princes Risborough Railway in an operational condition, but 37902 was reduced to scrap in 2005. 15 March 1992.

The next few images are from the Westbury area again, but this time freight is the main focus. The area has been quite a hot spot for the class over the years. 33009 and 33047 look very smart in 'Dutch' civil engineers' livery, which looked good when clean, as they come slowly through the station with the empty 6V96 09.38 Tonbridge to Meldon Quarry ballast train. 33009 and 33047 were both disposed of in 1997. 19 March 1991.

Four months later, and another 'Dutch' pair, this time 33026 and 33103, have charge of 6V96, the 09,38 Tonbridge to Meldon Quarry empty ballast train, and are seen at the same spot as the previous image. 33026 was scrapped in 2003, but 33103 is happily still with us and based at the Ecclesbourne Valley Railway, currently in engineers' plain grey livery. 24 July 1991.

This time we see the corresponding train, 6O74, the 11.20 Meldon Quarry to Tonbridge Yard loaded ballast, pulling up beside the station with the combination of 33026 *Seafire* and 33118, again both in civil engineers' 'Dutch' livery. Both of these locos have since been scrapped, 33026 in 2003 and 33118 in 1997. 8 April 1992.

Seafire

This is 33208 arriving in the up yard with a rake of HEA coal wagons on an unidentified working, but possibly bound for either Exmouth Junction (Exeter) or Yeovil Junction, both of which had terminals at the time for household coal conveyed in these type of wagons. The details for this loco were outlined earlier in the book. Circa 1990.

Left: The civil engineers 'Dutch' livery was quite new as we see 33057 running round its train in the down yard. Happily, this loco is now preserved on the West Somerset Railway and is in working order in BR green livery. 2 November 1990.

Below: Darkening the sky as it gets away from platform one, this is 33011 with a Cardiff Central to Portsmouth Harbour service. This loco was another of the earlier withdrawals, being taken out of service in 1989 and scrapped in 1990. Circa 1988.

Seen at the same platform as the previous shot, ready to depart this time is 33029 with another Cardiff Central to Portsmouth Harbour train. It was far more fortunate than the loco in the last shot, however, being withdrawn by BR in 1997. Amazingly, it can still be seen on the main line to this day working for WCRC usually based at its depot at Southall. 5 April 1988.

To conclude this short sequence at Westbury, we see 33019 drawing up to the departure line next to the station with a train of old track panels. After a short time based at Motherwell Depot for EWS in the early 2000s, though never actually active, this is another loco that has survived. Although it has been moved from one owner to another over the years, as mentioned earlier, I don't think it has actually worked in preservation as yet. 19 March 1991.

From a location that the class were common to one that you would have been hard pushed to have predicted back then! This is sole EWS-liveried 33030 in the yard at Aberdeen, of all places. Three locos (33019/025/030) were sent to Scotland in 1999 and based at Motherwell Depot, but 33025/030 were usually to be found at Aberdeen, where they were occasionally used on local freight trains in the area and for shunting. This arrangement did not last long, however, and the locos were withdrawn in 2001, then 025/030 moved to Direct Rail Services at the end of that year. DRS occasionally used them on flask trains until 2005, when both were sold on again, this time to WCRC. 33030 remains to this day at the company's base at Carnforth and is used as spares for three other members of the class. 28 February 2000.

The other loco of the trio that was based at Motherwell for a short time was 33025 (formerly *Sultan*), and it too could usually be found at Aberdeen, where it is seen stabled in the company of 33030. Its more recent history was similar to 33030, but unlike that loco, it is still active on the main line to this day, often operating together with 33029, both with WCRC. 28 February 2000.

Back in the south of England now. With a nice rake of matching liveried coaches, NSE 33114 *Ashford 150* gets away from Eastleigh station with 5R55, the 14.00 Eastleigh Depot to Salisbury empty stock working, which later formed the 15.13 service from Salisbury to London Waterloo. This loco, one of two to receive NSE livery, was scrapped during 1997. 7 October 1992.

Just over a week later, 33114 *Ashford 150* is seen stabled in the bay platform at Salisbury, present in the area in conjunction with a charter train. 15 October 1992.

The first now of a series of images showing the Class 33/1s at work on the Bournemouth to Weymouth line push-pull trains for which they were designed. This is 33101 hauling the usual Class 491 4-TC (later Class 438) units that form a London Waterloo to Weymouth train drifting down the gradient from Bincombe Tunnel towards Upwey near to journey's end. This loco was scrapped during 1997. 25 November 1987.

Near to where the last image was taken, this is 33111 bursting out from Bincombe Tunnel with another Waterloo to Weymouth service. This loco has fared much better, being secured for preservation during 1992. It has been based on the Swanage Railway, just a short distance away from its former stamping ground, since 2008. It can be a valuable asset when the line's steam locomotives are out of action or for use on engineering trains. 23 November 1987.

Moving up to Baiter, just east of Poole station, and we see 33105 pushing its Weymouth to London Waterloo train up the incline towards Parkstone. Poole Park boating lake can just be glimpsed to the left of the picture, and the land to the right was once part of Poole Harbour itself with the sea coming right up to the line, which was on a low concrete embankment before land reclamation in the early 1970s. Note also the early signs of third rail electrification, with conductor rail insulator pots in place. The loco was withdrawn in 1987 due to accident damage and was scrapped during 1990. 30 August 1986.

We are now at Keysworth Crossing, between Holton Heath and Wareham, as 33112 hauls 4-TC units 420 and 409 that form a London Waterloo to Weymouth service. Once again, conductor rail insulator pots can be seen scattered around. This loco succumbed to the scrapper's torch during 1992, again after a minor accident. 26 July 1986.

Propelling away from the brief stop at Holton Heath station, 33115 and 416 are heading for the next stop at Hamworthy forming a Weymouth to London Waterloo service. The train would have joined with either another 4-TC and 4-REP or just a 4-REP at Bournemouth for the continuation to London, while the '33' would come off and be ready to take another train down to Weymouth later in the day. This loco later went on to be an unpowered vehicle renumbered 83301 and painted in InterCity livery, becoming a test bed for Eurostar bogies and semi-permanently coupled to Class 73/2 73205. The former '33' was eventually scrapped in 1994. 14 July 1985.

Heading in the other direction and passing through Holton Heath non-stop are 33115 and 33119, with a Waterloo to Weymouth service. It was quite rare to see two locos on these trains and was probably brought about for the need of an extra loco at Weymouth for some reason. 20 September 1986.

Another shot taken during my time on the railway, this is 33114 hauling 4-TC sets 8025 and 8029 away from Moreton with a London Waterloo to Weymouth service. Just behind the camera is the point where the line was singled for the next seven miles or so to Dorchester South during 1985. The loco was scrapped in 1997. 27 November 1987.

This time we see 33118 pushing its formation of two 4-TC units away from Branksome towards its next stop at Bournemouth, where power would then be provided by a Class 430 4-REP unit, with a Weymouth to London Waterloo service. This loco was scrapped in early 1997. 18 March 1987.

33118 is seen again, this time near to the long closed Monkton & Came Halt, just south of Dorchester, with a London Waterloo to Weymouth service. The conductor rails are in place, and the big 'switch on' of power is just a few months away now. 22 November 1987.

An image now impossible to replicate in more ways than one. This view of 33113 and 33116 was taken from the long-demolished Branksome signal box and shows the locos coming from the lines that lead to Bournemouth Depot out onto the main line. This was originally the route that, after about a mile or so, eventually reached Bournemouth West station, which was closed and demolished during the late 1960s and was the terminus for trains off the Somerset & Dorset line, as well as terminating trains from London Waterloo like the famous all Pullman 'Bournemouth Belle'. 33113 was scrapped in 1997, but 33116 is still with us and can currently be found in operational condition on the Great Central Railway. 5 November 1986.

To finish this look at the Bournemouth to Weymouth section, we have four shots from the final weekday of regular Class 33/1 operation. This is 33106 hauling 4-TC 8021 and passing Redbridge (near Moreton) with a London Waterloo to Weymouth service. Part of the former Winfrith nuclear establishment can just be made out in the distance. This loco was scrapped in 1992. 13 May 1988.

The return service of the train seen in the previous shot is captured powering away from the Moreton stop with 33106 propelling 4-TC 8021 over the level crossing, heading for the next stop at Wool. 13 May 1988.

Making a fine sight at Redbridge (near Moreton), this is 33114 *Sultan* pushing 4-TCs 8028 and 8004 on a Weymouth to Waterloo service. Unit 8004 had only recently been painted in Network SouthEast livery at this time. The loco was scrapped in 1997. 13 May 1988.

This last image from that Friday back in 1988 sees 33101 and 8020 arriving at the Moreton stop with a London Waterloo to Weymouth train, complete with a makeshift headboard commemorating the end of 21 years of push-pull operation. This loco was scrapped in 1997. 13 May 1988.

Left: Another route that Class 33s were regularly seen on was the Bristol to Weymouth line, and here we see 33010 approaching Clink Road Junction at Frome in rapidly fading daylight with 2O60, the 16.15 Bristol Temple Meads to Weymouth service. This loco was scrapped during 1989. 14 March 1987.

Below: A little further south than the previous shot and we see 33101 hauling two 4-TC units on the approach to Bruton with 2V62, the 09.53 Saturdays-only Weymouth to Bristol Temple Meads service. 17 September 1988.

Further south still, at Maiden Newton, we find 33108 approaching with 2V63, the 10.30 Weymouth to Bristol Temple Meads hauling two 4-TC units, while waiting for them to clear the single line is 47566 with a Saturdays-only service bound for Weymouth. Since the late 2010s, services on this line have been operated mainly by Great Western Class 165/166 'Turbo' units with the occasional appearance of a Class 158. 33108 was subsequently preserved, and after spending a few years working on the Swanage Railway, it can now be found on the Severn Valley Railway. The Class 47 was scrapped during 2006. 9 September 1989.

Right: Just south of Westbury, near Witham Friary, we see 33040 passing with 6074, the 11.20 Meldon Quarry to Tonbridge Yard loaded ballast train; very often, these trains were double-headed, as can be seen in the next shot. This loco was reduced to scrap during 1997. Circa 1988.

Below: A little further along the line towards Westbury, we see the 'Dutch'-liveried duo 33103 and 33057 at Lambert's Bridge with the same 6074, the 11.20 Meldon Quarry to Tonbridge Yard loaded ballast train, but this time with a slightly larger load. Happily, both of these locos are still with us, with 33103 being based on the Ecclesbourne Valley Railway and 33057 on the West Somerset Railway. 14 September 1990.

Moving to the Westbury to Salisbury line now at Upton Scudamore, and we see 33010 powering up the gruelling incline that made even a four- or five-coach train seem heavy, with 1041, the 12.06 Cardiff Central to Portsmouth Harbour that the loco had worked from Bristol Temple Meads. This is thought to have been this loco's final passenger working, as it was withdrawn from service just 13 days later with electrical problems and scrapped during 1989. 5 April 1988.

Left: A couple of images now from the West Country, which was yet another area that the class could regularly be found. This is 'Slim Jim' 33204 at Exeter St Davids, having just arrived with 1V12, the 11.12 Brighton to Paignton. It was about to be uncoupled, with a fresh loco working forward to Paignton. 1 August 1987.

Below: At the same spot on the same day, we see Bournemouth to Weymouth push-pull fitted 33117 coming up the gradient with 1036, the 10.10 Cardiff Central to Portsmouth Harbour service. It was unusual, but not rare, to see Class 33/1s on these services. This loco is another survivor and can be found on the East Lancashire Railway. 5 April 1988.

With another Class 33, two Class 31s, two Class 47s and a first-generation Diesel Multiple Unit (DMU) on view in the former steam shed area, 33011 is seen waiting to exit the yard at Exeter St Davids. This location is still used for the intended purpose today, with a brand-new servicing depot having come into use during 2021 that cost a mind-boggling £56 million! 2 August 1986.

Winding their way out of the sidings just east of Exeter St Davids are 33010 and 33114, which will form 1O21, the 12.20 Exeter St Davids to London Waterloo service. These locos had both worked in on an earlier service from Waterloo and were undoubtedly deputising for an unavailable Class 50 loco. 2 August 1986.

These locos were so useful that they were often used by the former Western Region of BR for some of their internal services in the West Country. This is 33034 with just such a service from Paignton to Exeter St Davids, seen getting underway from Starcross station. Hard to believe that even this shot is now totally blocked by bushes these days. This loco lingered on for many years after withdrawal from service, until finally being scrapped on site at Norden on the Swanage Railway in January 2013. Circa 1986.

The second recipient of that unmistakeable nameplate, 'Slim Jim' 33207 *Earl Mountbatten of Burma* heads south through Kensington Olympia with a short train consisting of a couple of china clay tanks that originated at Quidhampton (near Salisbury) earlier in the day. This loco is still in main line service to this day with WCRC. 4 June 1996.

And this is the original recipient. 33027 *Earl Mountbatten of Burma* waits to depart Yeovil Junction with an Exeter St Davids to London Waterloo service. This loco was scrapped during 1992, and the nameplates transferred to the loco seen in the previous image. 19 October 1986.

33108 in 'Dutch' livery is captured passing through Southampton Central with the 6V38 Marchwood to Eastleigh Yard Ministry of Defence (MoD) train. Another loco that is still with us today, it is currently based on the Severn Valley Railway. 20 June 1991.

The final rays of sunshine at Gillingham this time as 33028 arrives with 1O16, the 13.45 Exeter St Davids to Waterloo service. This loco was scrapped during 1989. 26 October 1986.

From the West Country up to Manchester Piccadilly for this shot as we see 33023 waiting to depart with 1V05, the 13.45 to Cardiff Central. Although this loco was sold to Harry Needle Railroad Company (HNRC) after withdrawal from service, it was never restored and finally cut up during 2005. 7 August 1985.

The driver looks back for the all clear as 33003 waits to depart Poole with an inter-regional train for the north of England. Even in later years, the Class 33s appeared occasionally on these trains, quite often due to the failure of the rostered Class 47 before departure. This loco was badly damaged in an accident during 1987 and was scrapped as a result. Circa 1986.

To conclude this first section of this book, we see the only other member of the class to receive Network SouthEast livery apart from 33114 *Ashford 150*. This is 33035 *Spitfire* stabled in the holding sidings at Eastleigh. This was the second loco to receive this name after 33047 was withdrawn from service. 2 March 1994.

Chapter 2

Main Lines 2001–Present

While most of the fleet were withdrawn by the dawn of the new millennium, others were starting fresh careers for new operators. This section portrays some of the duties for which they have been used up to the present time, mostly with WCRC in more recent times, as it is the only operator that currently (in 2022) uses the class on the main line.

During the early part of the new millennium, various members of the fleet were used by Fragonset Railways (since disbanded) to haul the new Desiro units that were about to enter service for South West Trains, replacing the old slam-door trains. Some of these new units were hauled by Class 33s to/from various locations for testing with one place being Weymouth, where a purpose-built compound with an inspection pit was provided. The new units often conducted night-time testing between Wareham and Weymouth. This is 33108 *Vampire* hauling brand new Class 450 450019 and various barrier vehicles through Eastleigh bound for Weymouth, with 33103 *Swordfish* out of sight on the rear. 26 June 2003.

A couple of weeks later, and a similar ensemble, this time with 33103 *Swordfish* leading, is seen heading away from Poole at Baiter, probably bound for Northam Depot, near Southampton. 8 July 2003.

This is 33103 *Swordfish* hauling another new Desiro through Southampton Central heading south on an unidentified working but probably with the destination being either Bournemouth or Weymouth. Circa 2003.

SWORDFISH

Eastleigh

Privately-owned but hired to Fragonset Railways, 33021 *Eastleigh* was another loco used on these moves and is seen here approaching Millbrook with just the barrier coaches and wagons this time, heading for Eastleigh Yard. This loco has since re-entered preservation on the Churnet Valley Railway. 11 September 2003.

Occasionally, rather than a loco on each end of these unit moves, both were on the front. This is 33103 *Swordfish* and 33021 *Eastleigh* heading north through the series of bridges on the approach to Winchester, hauling an unidentified Desiro Class 450 unit. 15 May 2003.

By late 2003, most of these unit moves were finished, and the locos used to haul them left the Bournemouth area for pastures new. This is 33103 *Swordfish*, 33108 *Vampire* and 33021 *Eastleigh* stabled by the signalling centre building at Westbury during a layover. All these locos later entered preservation proper. 8 October 2003.

33202 *Meteor* also saw use hauling units, but it is seen here stabled between duties at Clapham Junction. The loco is currently based on the Mid Norfolk Railway. 10 July 2003.

These Fragonset examples also saw regular use on charter trains, often as support locos for the main steam loco rostered for haulage. 33103 *Swordfish* is seen breasting the summit of the southbound climb to Beaulieu Road station in the New Forest National Park with the Alton to Poole empty stock for the 1Z80 08.33 Poole to Bristol Temple Meads, hauled by ex-BR Standard 5 73096, which was on the rear at this point. 22 September 2004.

This train was originally to have been hauled by West Country Pacific 34016 *Bodmin* and Standard Class 5 73096, but 33202 *Meteor* was a last-minute substitute because of a late notice steam ban. With quite a few happy punters despite the lack of steam haulage, the loco is seen powering past the former Poole signal box (since demolished) with 1Z93, the 07.15 Alton to Weymouth 'The Weymouth Boat Train' organised by Daylight Railtours. This stock was often referred to as the 'Green Train', the predominately Mk.2 set being finished in Southern green. 23 August 2003.

A few months later, and 33202 *Meteor* was used on another charter. It is seen coming up the incline towards Bruton station (Somerset) with 1Z96, the 07.59 Yeovil Junction to London Victoria 'The Sussex Sulzer/London Excursion' organised by Pathfinder Tours. This was a thoroughly wet and miserable day, and the rain literally never let up! 22 November 2003.

Based on the Swanage Railway, 33012 was main line registered in the late 2000s and has proved a very useful loco over the years. The immaculate machine (then not carrying a name) is seen approaching Wareham with an interesting consist of 73136 *Perseverance*, 73205 *Jeanette* and 3-CIG unit 1498 *Farringford* running as 5Z73, the 12.15 Bournemouth Depot to Swanage to take part in the upcoming diesel gala. 73136 has since returned to main line use with GB Railfreight (GBRf), and 73205 has been rebuilt and re-engined by GBRf to become 73964. 5 May 2011.

Three years later, and 33012 (still un-named) was working a similar move, this time hauling 50026 *Indomitable*, 50031 *Hood* and 73207 as 0Z33, the 11.33 Eastleigh Works to Swanage for the line's 2014 diesel gala. 73207 has since been rebuilt as 73971 and now operates just about as far away as you can get from its original stamping ground in the Highlands of Scotland working Caledonian Sleeper services! 7 May 2014.

Another trip out for 33012 (this time named *Lt Jenny Lewis RN*) as we see it pulling away from a brief stop at Brockenhurst with 5Z12, the 10.13 Swanage to Eastleigh Works, hauling the Swanage-based DMU that was going for a total refurbishment to main line standards. 18 September 2014.

Such was the slack timings for this run, I was able to get on a train from Brockenhurst to Southampton Airport Parkway to get this further shot approaching the station. 18 September 2014.

For the past 15 years or so, the main operator of Class 33s on the main line has been WCRC and most of the remainder of this section of the book portrays a selection of its small fleet in action. This is 33029 *Glen Loy* at Westbury with an unusual duty hauling restored 'Lord Nelson' Class 850 *Lord Nelson* from the West Somerset Railway as 5Z46 Bishops Lydeard to Heywood (East Lancashire Railway), a move that must have taken a very long time! 23 November 2006.

At the time of writing, 33207 *Jim Martin* is the only main line-registered Class 33/2 and is seen departing Eastleigh hauling a large Kirow crane as the short distance 6Z33 11.11 Eastleigh Yard to Totton Yard. 21 March 2014.

Glen Loy

A few months earlier and it was 33029 *Glen Loy* on crane haulage duty (the same crane perhaps?). It is seen departing Westbury with 6Z47, the 10.46 Westbury to Woking, which was routed via Reading and Guildford. 9 January 2014.

33025 and 37516 make for an unusual combination as they haul the London Underground-liveried 4-TC unit on the approach to Mortimer (on the Basingstoke to Reading line) running as 5Z21, the 07.10 Swanage to West Ruislip LUL Depot. The locos and stock were returning after use on the Swanage to Wareham shuttle services that operated during the year. 4 September 2017.

Another unusual move, this time for a solo 33025 seen at Basingstoke with 5Z46, the 13.37 Eastleigh Works to Southall, with an assortment of rather battered-looking ex-Southern Railway EMU vehicles in tow. 12 August 2021.

Left: A few shots now of the popular 1Z33, the 05.58 Crewe to Weymouth 'The Dorset Coast Explorer and Great Wey Round' charter organised by Pathfinder Tours that utilised 33207 *Jim Martin* and 33025 *Glen Falloch* throughout. The first view sees the train heading south along the Castle Cary to Yeovil Pen Mill single line at Dimmer, just south of Castle Cary. 23 August 2008.

Below: Luckily, the train had some very generous timings, and I was able to get ahead of it to capture this shot of the pair as they thread their way up through the approach cutting, about to enter Bincombe Tunnel. Part of the Dorset county town of Dorchester can be seen in the background. 23 August 2008.

On arrival at Weymouth, the two locos were shunted around so that 33207 could lead again for the later departure north. The differing bodyside profiles of the locos are quite apparent in this shot in Jersey Sidings. 23 August 2008.

The last shot of this charter sees the duo crossing the causeway at Holes Bay, between Hamworthy and Poole. 23 August 2008.

This was one of the early charters involving the newly acquired WCRC Class 33s. Immaculate 33025, standing patiently at Bognor Regis, is about to have its moment of glory hauling 1Z83, the 14.18 Bognor Regis to London Victoria 'Sussex Belle' organised by the Railway Touring Company. The main tour loco was Bulleid 'Battle of Britain' Pacific 34067 *Tangmere,* which was at the buffer stops, but, as there were no turning facilities for the loco at Bognor Regis, the '33' headed the train the short distance to Littlehampton, from where the steam loco took over for the remainder of the run to London Victoria. 23 September 2006.

Not long after departure from Bognor Regis, 33025 is seen powering towards Ford station with 34067 *Tangmere* hanging on at the rear. It was a great pity about the kaleidoscope of colours that made up the coaching stock though! 23 September 2006.

Two former Southern Region stalwarts are seen here on the Great Western Main Line at Tilehurst as 33029 and 34067 *Tangmere* head east with 5Z40, the 10.35 Bristol Kingsland Road to Southall WCRC empty stock move. 18 August 2014.

A heavy load and a very gloomy morning for 33029 as it passes the autumn colours and 70001 stabled at Southampton Maritime Depot, with 5Z89, the 10.12 Poole to Southall, and 'Black 5' 44871 on the rear. This was returning empty stock from a charter run the day before with the steam loco. 29 November 2013.

As we have already seen, Class 33s have often been used to assist with steam charters, and this is the first of a few shots showing 33207 *Jim Martin* as tail gunner. It is seen passing Hawkeridge Junction, just north of Westbury, on the rear of 1Z82, the 07.12 London Victoria to Cardiff Central 'The Cathedrals Express/St David's Day' organised by Steam Dreams, which was hauled by 'Black Five' 44932. 1 March 2014.

This time we see the loco at Salisbury, having just arrived on the rear of 1Z92, the 08.43 London Victoria to Yeovil Junction 'The Sherborne Christmas Carol' organised by the Railway Touring Company. The main tour engine was BR Standard 'Britannia' Pacific 70013 *Oliver Cromwell*. 14 December 2017.

During 2019, there were a series of steam-hauled trips from London Waterloo using ex-London North Eastern Railway B1 61306 *Mayflower* to Windsor & Eton Riverside and return. 33207 *Jim Martin* was often used as the support loco and also headed the trains on the return from Windsor. This is the loco departing London Waterloo on the rear of the first train of the day, 1Z80, the 08.05 to Windsor & Eton Riverside. 13 August 2019.

Our last shot of 33207 *Jim Martin* bringing up the rear sees it passing Wardour (just west of Tisbury) with 1Z67, the 09.00 London Waterloo to Yeovil Junction leg of 'The End of Southern Steam' charter organised by the Railway Touring Company. This was running almost exactly 50 years to the day that steam operations finished on BR's Southern Region on 9 July 1967, and the main tour loco was 34046 *Braunton* (running at the time as 34052 *Lord Dowding*). 8 July 2017.

33012 (D6515) *Lt Jenny Lewis RN* stands at Yeovil Pen Mill on an interesting working. At the other end of this train is the Swanage Railway's U Class 2-6-0 steam loco 31806, which had just come up from Weymouth on its main line debut with this test run, the 5Z42 12.20 Swanage to Yeovil Pen Mill via Weymouth. This was the first time one of these steam locos had been seen on the main line for 54 years! The train is about to head up to Yeovil Junction so the steam loco could be coaled and watered. 13 April 2018.

Left: 33012 *Lt Jenny Lewis RN* departs Yeovil Junction on the rear of the train heading back to Yeovil Pen Mill, from where it would later head the train back to Weymouth with the steam loco on the rear. 13 April 2018.

Below: Another first! 33012 *Lt Jenny Lewis RN* has just arrived at Wareham with an empty stock train from Swanage. The first couple of trains on this day were for Swanage Railway members and officials, but later in the day, this loco (along with 37518 on the other end) worked the first public service train (not a charter) between Wareham and Swanage since 2 January 1972. As can be seen, there was certainly a lot of interest around the station! 13 June 2017.

33012 *Lt Jenny Lewis RN* is seen again, this time departing Basingstoke hauling London Underground's 4-TC as 1Z82, the 09.02 London Waterloo to Warminster 'By Routemaster to the Lost Village of Imber' charter organised by UK Railtours. Imber is a village on Salisbury Plain that was taken over by the military many years ago and is usually off limits to the public. The Routemaster part of the title refers to the fact that participants had the option to travel to the village from the closest station at Warminster by an old London bus. 73107 *Tracy* was on the rear of the train throughout. 17 August 2019.

Right: After 33207 ran round the train had and taken a short trip to Yeovil Pen Mill, the charter is seen arriving back into Yeovil Junction with 33012 leading, from where the train continued west in top and tail mode. 8 March 2020.

Below: The first of a few shots of another interesting tour as we now move to the lovely Somerset countryside, where we see 33207 *Jim Martin* and 33012 *Lt Jenny Lewis RN* near Milborne Port as they are about to descend the incline down to Sherborne with 1Z38, the 09.38 London Victoria to Coleford Junction (near Crediton) via a quick detour down the short distance from Yeovil Junction to Yeovil Pen Mill, entitled 'The Devonian Crompton' organised by the Branch Line Society. 8 March 2020.

Due to late running service trains, the charter finally left Yeovil Junction around 45 minutes late, although much of this was made up with not having to cross any other service trains to Exeter. 33012 awaits the off at Yeovil Junction just as the rain starts falling. 8 March 2020.

33207 is seen departing Yeovil Junction bringing up the rear of the train. It was a quick dash for cover after this! As it turned out, this was one of the last charters to operate for a few months, as a few days later, the UK was in lockdown when the COVID-19 pandemic struck, throwing everything into chaos. 8 March 2020.

Still in Somerset, we now see 33029 passing Wyke Champflower, just south of Bruton, with 1Z33, the 05.27 Crewe to Weymouth 'The Marching Crompton II' organised by the Branch Line Society. 47851 was on the rear at this point, and the return from Weymouth was double-headed by 33012 *Lt Jenny Lewis RN* and 33029 all the way back to Crewe with 47851 still on the rear. Swanage-based 33012 ran light engine from Swanage to Weymouth to join this tour. 23 March 2019.

Not exactly an everyday sight along the sea wall these days! This is 33207 *Jim Martin* and 37706 working 0Z47, the 10.22 Plymouth to Theale Loop past Dawlish. The locos had worked to Plymouth earlier on 1Z47, the 08.35 Penzance to Plymouth, from where steam locos 45596 *Bahamas* and 61306 *Mayflower* then worked the train on to London Victoria via a water stop at Norton Fitzwarren. 1 October 2021.

Later the same day, 33207 *Jim Martin* and 37706 are seen here lurking in the weed-infested bay platform at Taunton station. When the two steam locos had coaled and watered, the two diesels departed just ahead of the charter to Theale Loop, then followed the charter to London Victoria to take the whole train empty back to Southall Depot. 1 October 2021.

This is 33029 just south of St Denys, hauling the LUL 4-TC as 1Z33, the 10.24 Ealing Broadway to Swanage 'The Purbeck Explorer I' organised by the Swanage Railway. This tour was originally intended to be hauled by a Class 20 and was used to get the 4-TC unit to the Swanage Railway for its diesel gala. Apart from the liveries, this is quite authentic, as back in BR days, a Class 33/0 could often be seen substituting for a Class 33/1 in hauling 4-TC units. 7 May 2014.

Glen Falloch

Here we see 33025 *Glen Falloch* arriving at Weymouth station with 1Z82, the 09.41 Waterloo to Weymouth intriguingly named 'Dorset Dumpling' charter, organised by Spitfire Railtours. 73136 *Perseverance* was on the other end of the train and lead on departure north later in the day. 6 September 2008.

To round off this section, things are brought right up to date as we see 33029 and 33025 passing Wyke Champflower, just north of Castle Cary, with 1Z34, the 16.35 Weymouth to Burton upon Trent 'Dorset Coast Explorer' charter organised by Pathfinder Tours. 6 August 2022.

Just one week later, and the same pair were out on the main line again, this time standing in at short notice for Jubilee 4-6-0 45596 *Bahamas* due to a Network Rail steam ban. The train is 1Z50, the 07.13 London Paddington to Minehead (West Somerset Railway), seen topping the sharp gradient at North Brewham, just east of Bruton. Class 33s were used on this particular train as they could work over the whole distance of the West Somerset Railway, as there is still a restriction on heavier locos in place on the line. 13 August 2022.

Chapter 3

On Heritage Lines

With 25 of the class preserved in various states of restoration, it is more than evident that they are still proving very popular and are useful additions to many heritage lines around the country, especially when these lines find themselves short of steam locos. This section looks at a few locos at work on lines in the south of England, with an emphasis on the Swanage Railway in Dorset.

Right: The Mid Hants (Watercress Line) has made good use of the class over the years, although there are no examples currently based there. This is 33053, which was resident for a few years, climbing the gradient away from Ropley with an Alton-bound train. This loco can now be found on the Battlefield Line in Leicestershire. 29 May 2009.

Below: Later in the day, the sun had come round to the other side of the line, and 33053 is seen near the same location as the previous image with another train bound for Alton. 29 May 2009.

A loco that was based on the Mid Hants for some years was 33208, and during its time there it was registered for main line running during the late 1990s/early 2000s. The loco is seen departing Ropley with 47306 *The Sapper* heading for Alton during the line's popular diesel gala, dubbed as 'The Trainspotters Ball'! This is another loco that can now be found on the Battlefield Line but not currently in an operational state. 27 April 2002.

33208 is seen again, this time framed by the bridge on the approach to Alresford with a train from Alton. The '99' shown in the headcode box used to refer to the Brighton to Exeter train that ran back in BR days. 27 April 2002.

The following year, the Mid Hants held its diesel gala a month later, and one of the visiting locos was another 'Slim Jim' in the guise of 33201. This is yet another example based on the Battlefield Line, but is seen here having just arrived at Medstead & Four Marks with an Alton-bound train looking very smart in its BR green livery. 16 May 2003.

Another view of 33201 while it awaited departure, allowing a good view of the wonderful old signal box that stood at Wilton South Station, just west of Salisbury. The box closed in the early 1980s and was removed and rebuilt here at Medstead & Four Marks soon after. 16 May 2003.

Another loco to have made a few visits to the line over the years is 33109 *Captain Bill Smith RNR,* and during one of its most recent appearances, it was paired up with preserved 4-VEP 3417 *Gordon Pettitt,* making for an authentic look. Class 33/1s did occasionally work with 4-VEPs (and other EMUs) in BR days. The loco is seen on a gloomy day hauling the 4-VEP as they coast down the bank towards Ropley with an Alresford-bound train. Note the loco is sporting white window surrounds, a touch that harks back to the Class 33/1s final days on the Bournemouth to Weymouth push-pull trains, when a few examples unofficially received these embellishments. 26 April 2013.

A rather unusual, model-like, broadside view of the same combination is seen a little further east towards Medstead & Four Marks, also heading for Alresford. 26 April 2013.

On one of its earlier visits, 33109 *Captain Bill Smith RNR* (carrying its original D6525 number) is seen at Medstead & Four Marks with Freightliner Class 57/0 57011 *Freightliner Challenger* as pilot loco. The Class 57 was, at the time, the most recent conversion, formerly 47329. This gala was a convenient way of running the loco in and providing punters with an unusual loco for haulage. 4 March 2000.

During its visit to the line for the annual diesel gala, the pairing of two 'Slim Jims' was obviously going to happen at some point! This is 33201 and 33208 thundering away from Ropley with a train for Alton. Note the different shades of green the locos are wearing. 18 May 2003.

When I paid a random visit to the line in early 2008, I was delighted to find that the DMU rostered for the day's services had developed some sort of engine trouble (apologies to DMU fans out there!), and so 33208 was attached to give a helping hand. The loco is seen pulling away from the stop at Ropley with a train for Alton. 2 February 2008.

By the following year, the loco was starting to look rather tired, with quite a bit of rust and holes appearing in the bodywork. The loco is seen stabled on the shed at Ropley with an equally tired BR Standard Class 4 2-6-0 steam loco 76017. 13 March 2009.

We now move away from the Mid Hants line to the Swanage Line in South Dorset, which as mentioned forms the bulk of this section. Firstly, a couple of early views of 33012 *Stan Symes* in action as we see the loco without a yellow warning panel coming across Corfe Viaduct and approaching Norden with a demonstration goods train. 26 November 2000.

The same demonstration goods train is seen again, this time arriving in to Harmans Cross station on the same day. 26 November 2000.

A few years later, and 33012 *Stan Symes* has now gained a yellow panel as it powers under Townsend farm bridge on Corfe Castle Common while heading for Swanage with a train from Norden. 31 March 2007.

This time the loco is arriving at Swanage with a train from Norden. Although it appears to have always been there, the signal box seen in the background was almost new at this time, being opened during 2003 and replacing the original one that stood almost opposite, which was closed and demolished in 1967. 8 July 2006.

Some lovely autumn light this time as the loco enters Corfe Castle station with a Norden to Swanage train. This was taken during the line's member's day, which is no longer held. 27 November 2005.

This time a fine early spring day sees the loco crossing Corfe Viaduct with a Norden to Swanage service. This image was taken from the mound Corfe Castle itself sits on and is an excellent vantage point to watch proceedings on the railway; during the spring and summer it abounds with wild orchids. Shame about that red Mk.1 brake van! 1 April 2005.

Since the installation of the former Merton Park (near Wimbledon) station footbridge at Corfe Castle in 2007, this is the fine view that can be had of Norden to Swanage trains entering the station. 33012, by now renamed *Lt Jenny Lewis RN*, arrives into the down platform on a fine early summer morning bound for Swanage. 8 June 2019.

After a recent overhaul and repaint, the loco looks spotless as it comes round the curve off Corfe Common and approaches the station at Corfe Castle with a train for Norden during the ever-popular diesel gala. Visiting 37503 can be seen attached to the rear of the train. 7 May 2011.

Almost exactly 11 years separates this shot from the previous one, and it is taken at the same location, albeit looking in the other direction. After another overhaul and repaint, the loco looks even more immaculate as it heads a Norden to Swanage train just after departing Corfe Castle. It is interesting to note that the window surrounds and body stripe are actually white, as opposed to the creamy brown colour back in the 2011 shot. 6 May 2022.

33012 *Lt Jenny Lewis RN* and 33201 are seen paired up as they approach Norden during the line's 2016 gala. The 'Slim Jim' was visiting from the Battlefield Line. These green/blue loco combinations were relatively common back in the early 1970s. 6 May 2016.

Another loco to have put in good service on the line was 33103 *Swordfish*, which has kept its name bestowed upon it during its days working on the main line for Fragonset Railways. The resplendent Rail Blue loco is seen in the sunshine at Harmans Cross with a train for Norden. The loco is no longer main line-registered and has since moved on to the Ecclesbourne Valley Railway and sports engineers' plain grey livery. 8 May 2009.

A mighty train for 33103 *Swordfish* this time, as the loco heads south at Afflington and towards Harmans Cross with the empty stock from a railtour originating in London that had arrived at Swanage earlier behind Bulleid Pacific 34067 *Tangmere*. As the train was far longer than the line usually deals with, the train was emptied of passengers at Swanage (which took some time!) then it had to go back up the line as ECS to beyond Norden to stable. Later in the day, as seen here, the stock was taken back to Swanage for a late afternoon departure, headed by 37706, which is attached to the rear at this point. With 34067 *Tangmere* on the rear from Swanage as far as Southampton, the train would then change direction to go via Andover to Basingstoke, with the Bulleid Pacific leading for the remainder of the journey back to London. 2 May 2009.

With the slack timings, I was able to get another shot of the stock as it arrived at Swanage behind the '33' and passing 34067 *Tangmere*, which had been serviced at Swanage shed. 2 May 2009.

This time engaged on more usual Swanage duties, the loco is captured crossing Corfe Viaduct as it heads another service from Norden to Swanage. 6 May 2011.

We now see the loco ticking over at Swanage as it awaits departure for Norden hauling green-liveried 3-CIG 1498 *Farringford*. The CIG unit last saw main line service on the Brockenhurst to Lymington line until May 2010, when it was replaced by other stock. Although it can be hauled by a loco, its use is limited on heritage railways as it requires the third rail to operate the lights and heating. Although the unit was based on the Epping to Ongar line for a while, it was exported to Ireland in October 2016 to become holiday accommodation at the Quirky Glamping Village at Enniscorne in County Sligo. 8 June 2011.

During this loco's stay at Swanage, it was always nice to see it paired up with 33111, which is also based on the line as we will see later. The pair are seen coming across Corfe Viaduct with a train for Norden. 7 November 2009.

The cows at Afflington seem far from impressed as 33103 *Swordfish* and 33111 pass by hauling 4-VEP 3417 *Gordon Pettitt* on a Swanage to Norden train. 7 May 2010.

Here is something a little different! 33108 is captured on the outskirts of Poole heading along the A35 Upton by-pass while being transported to the Swanage Railway. The loco had just been restored. Although there is no obvious sign, the once double-track line that left the Waterloo to Weymouth main line at Hamworthy Junction used to go across behind the loco to the left of the picture. This road was non-existent back then, with the area being just heathland with the line on a low embankment. It is just possible that this very loco may have travelled along it in its early days! 10 May 2005.

33108 worked on the Swanage Railway for a couple of years before moving on. The loco is seen on one of its early runs soon after departure from Norden on a service for Swanage. 12 June 2005.

In May 2013, the loco returned to the Swanage line for that year's diesel gala, which commemorated 25 years since the end of Class 33/1s on the Bournemouth to Weymouth push-pull trains. For this event, the loco received white window surrounds on one end only. Darkening the sky on departure from Corfe Castle, we see the loco heading for Swanage with a train from Norden. 10 May 2013.

Left: This is the loco at Swanage during a shunt manoeuvre with Class 55 'Deltic' 55019 *Royal Highland Fusilier*, something that would have been highly unlikely to have occurred during BR days. 11 May 2013.

Below: In 2013, this was about as close as you could get to a perfect reproduction of the 1980s push-pull scenario. This should change in the not-too-distant future when the 4-TC Group based at Swanage get its own unit currently under restoration (to be numbered 413) up and running. 33108 hauls 4-VEP 3417 *Gordon Pettitt* on the approach to Herston Halt with a Swanage-bound train. 12 May 2013.

Complete with what is believed to be the original makeshift headboard used back at the time, 33108 and 33111 are hauling 4-VEP 3417 *Gordon Pettitt* again as they cross Corfe Viaduct and approach their destination at Norden. 9 May 2013.

Another shot of the same pairing as they approach Harmans Cross station with a service for Swanage. 11 May 2013.

Not a good outcome for this particular loco, I'm afraid. 33034 was withdrawn from service during 1988 and was sold to a private buyer in 1990 and moved to MoD Ludgershall for storage. After a couple of changes of ownership while in storage, it finally moved to Swanage during 2001. The original intention was to fully restore the loco while here, but unfortunately parts were stolen from it and it was eventually deemed a hopeless case. It is seen at Norden actually looking quite presentable. 28 March 2004.

Left: In early 2013, the loco was looking in a very sorry state while in the process of being disposed of. All re-useable parts were being recovered before cutting commenced. 6 January 2013.

Below: A view of the other side of the loco finds the power unit has been removed and cutting has started. Note that the loco wore BR blue on one side and BR green on the other! 6 January 2013.

A final shot of the demise of 33034 as it is consigned to the history books. At least it must hold some sort of record for surviving 25 years between the time it was withdrawn and the time it was finally scrapped? 6 January 2013.

Right: Now we move on to 33111, which is another stalwart of the Swanage Railway, seeing service alongside 33012. The loco was purchased by the Class 33/1 Preservation Group in 1992, and after restoration went on loan to Swanage in 2008 where it remains to the present time. We see it here approaching the Woodyhyde Camp Site near Harmans Cross with a Norden to Swanage service. 13 May 2012.

Below: At some point, the loco received the unofficial painted-on name of *Hot Dog*! Looking nice and tidy, it is seen this time rounding the curve at Afflington with a Norden-bound service hauling 3-CIG 1498 *Farringford*. 19 November 2011.

After mentioning the close authenticity of the train earlier, this is another very close effort! If only this teak-liveried 4-TC unit was painted in BR blue/grey, it would be absolutely perfect. It is being hauled by 33111 approaching Afflington bridge, soon after leaving Harmans Cross, with a Swanage to Norden service. 11 May 2014.

On occasions when the Swanage Railway permanent way gang cut the area around Corfe Viaduct, it opens up this fine view as the loco comes across with a Swanage to Norden service. 28 December 2013.

In some nice clear winter light, the loco is seen departing Norden with a demonstration freight train heading for Swanage consisting of a fine selection of wagons. 27 December 2014.

High up on the Purbeck Hills that overlook the Swanage line, there are some great views to be had. Looking a bit like a model train, the loco has just departed Harmans Cross and is heading for Norden with a train from Swanage. 20 February 2010.

This time we see the loco just after departure from Herston Halt and about a mile or so from its destination with a Norden to Swanage train. The large grey building in the background behind the one with the angled roof is Herston Works, where much of the restoration work done on Swanage locos is undertaken. 27 March 2010.

Eleven years later, and the loco is looking very faded and tired as it leaves Harmans Cross for Swanage, hauling just one coach that it had picked up from the sidings. It must be overdue a repaint? 28 July 2021.

33111 and 33108 have just passed Quarr Farm level crossing and are approaching Harmans Cross with a Swanage to Norden service. 11 May 2013.

Left: 33111 has just been detached from 33012 *Stan Symes* upon arrival at Swanage with a train from Norden. This was one of 33111's first runs on the line and was yet to receive the BR emblems on its cabsides. 29 November 2008.

Below: Low winter lighting again enhances this shot of 33111 and 33012 *Lt Jenny Lewis RN* coming across Corfe Common with a Norden to Swanage train formed of just three coaches. It appears the 33111 might be doing all the work! 28 December 2018.

The next four images were all taken on the same day. It has always been the plan by the railway to get a Swanage to Wareham main line service up and running, but the delay in restoring the intended DMUs to operate this service has frustrated things somewhat. However, during the summer of 2017, a trial season was run under contract by WCRC using the London Underground's 4-TC set with a WCRC loco at each end. During this period of running, a couple of different locos were used. An obvious candidate was Swanage's own main line-registered 33012 *Lt Jenny Lewis RN* and it is seen approaching Grange Road, just south of Worgret Junction, with a Swanage to Wareham service. 13 August 2017.

The loco on the other end of the train was 33025, seen approaching the main Wareham to Swanage A351 road bridge, just north of Norden, with a Wareham to Swanage service. Although this section of line is operated by the Swanage Railway, it is not as yet used regularly. 13 August 2017.

33012 *Lt Jenny Lewis RN* makes a spirited getaway from Norden Gates with a Swanage to Wareham service. To the left of shot, work is underway to create a dedicated loading/unloading area for stock movements to/from the railway. 13 August 2017.

33025 looks immaculate as it approaches Creech Bottom Crossing, between Worgret Junction and Norden, with another Wareham to Swanage service. The '98' showing in the headcode box is correct, and it was used in the early 1970s prior to closure when DMUs or the occasional loco-hauled train used the line. 13 August 2017.

To conclude this series of images on the Swanage Railway, we see a couple more locos that have paid visits to the line. This is smart looking 'Slim Jim' 33201 approaching Quarr Farm Crossing with a demonstration freight train heading for Swanage. 28 December 2015.

33201 initially arrived on the line for the 2015 diesel gala but was given an extended visit to cover for one of the line's own '33s' that was out of service. The loco is seen passing the former oil terminal at Furzebrook with a Swanage to River Frome Bridge service. It is the Swanage Railway's hope that, in the not-too-distant future, it will take on these redundant sidings for much needed storage space. 7 May 2015.

Above: The loco has just departed Norden, this time with a short three coach train bound for Swanage. The '62' headcode displayed in the front blinds used to refer to the London Waterloo to Exeter route back in BR days, a line that this loco would have worked on many occasions over the years. 28 December 2015.

Right: 33201 and 33012 *Lt Jenny Lewis RN* are arriving at Harmans Cross with a train from Norden to Swanage. Casual visitors to the line probably have no idea that the signal box here only dates back to 1996, and the station itself to 1989. 6 May 2016.

Another popular visitor that enjoyed an extended stay was sister 'Slim Jim', 33202 *Dennis G. Robinson*. Superb morning light illuminates the loco as it departs Norden with a train for Swanage. 33111 is attached to the rear of the train. From this angle, it is very apparent how much narrower the '33/2' is than the Mk.1 coach directly behind it. 14 December 2013.

This is the loco arriving at Corfe Castle on a misty morning with a Norden to Swanage train. This was the year that the diesel gala remembered good old Network SouthEast, and various locations on the line were adorned with NSE-style running in boards and the like as a bit of fun, depicting what 'might have been' had the branch to Swanage not closed in 1972! 8 May 2014.

Left: There is certainly no mistaking this location as the loco arrives at Corfe Castle station with a Swanage to Norden train on a damp, gloomy winter's day. 14 December 2013.

Below: Further south, we see the 'Slim Jim' passing Woodyhyde with a Norden to Swanage train. Part of the Purbeck Hills can be glimpsed in the background. 11 May 2014.

Dennis G. Robinson

Captured right at the point of the token exchange between the signaller and loco crew, a Norden to Swanage train arrives at its destination behind the same loco again. 8 May 2014.

Right: On the same day as the previous shot, 33202 is again arriving into Swanage in the mist and gloom, but a little earlier in the day with a train from Norden. 8 May 2014.

Below: With a convenient lull in the almost continuous stream of traffic on the A351 in the foreground, we see 33202 *Dennis G. Robinson* crossing Corfe Viaduct not long after departing from Norden with a train for Swanage. 9 May 2014.

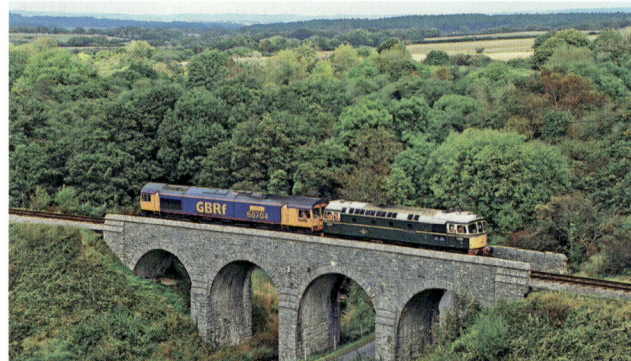

GBRf's 66704 *Colchester Power Signal Box* was the first main line loco to visit the Swanage line, bringing in a ballast train from Eastleigh as far as Norden. The loco was detached and later hauled to Swanage by 33012, seen here crossing Corfe Viaduct. While there was no real need for this move, it was thought the loco crews wanted to have lunch in Swanage! 10 October 2007.

Left: Eleven years later, and the same loco stands in the same spot, but renumbered back to its original D6501 identity and in BR green livery. It does still carry the *Sea King* nameplates that were first affixed in the early 1990s, though. Behind it is 37037, awaiting an overhaul. 30 August 2019.

Below: We now move onto the South Devon Railway for a few images. Looking very resplendent in civil engineers' 'Dutch' livery, this is 33002 *Sea King* stabled at Buckfastleigh. This is the oldest example of the class in preservation. 26 April 2008.

Right: Our old friend 33202 again, which paid a visit to the line back in 2008. Semaphore signals dominate as the loco is waiting to depart from Buckfastleigh with a train for Totnes Littlehempston. The signal box in the background is not actually in use, the active signal box is situated behind the camera at the station throat. 26 April 2008.

Below: Here it is again soon after departure from Buckfastleigh with a service to Totnes Littlehempston, hauling a DMU and masses of excited punters it seems. 26 April 2008.

Further along this delightful heritage line, we see the loco about to depart Staverton Halt with an afternoon train heading for Totnes Littlehempston. 26 April 2008.

At the time, a new signal box was under construction at Totnes Littlehempston and can be seen here at an advanced stage as 33202 is in the process of running round its train in the station, just out of view to the right of the picture. The signal box, which is now called Ashburton Junction, was originally located at Cradley Heath but was moved to the South Devon Railway in early 2004 and reconstructed on site. 26 April 2008.

The huge running in board on the platform leaves the viewer in no doubt that 33202 is awaiting departure with a train for Buckfastleigh. The station buildings here (behind the camera) used to be situated at Toller Porcorum on the Maiden Newton to Bridport branch line, but when that line closed in the mid-1970s, they were saved and moved lock, stock and barrel to here for reconstruction. 26 April 2008.

Another visitor to the line in 2003 was 33110, seen here in the process of running round its train at Buckfastleigh. 11 May 2003.

The loco now awaits departure from Buckfastleigh with a two coach train for Totnes Littlehempston. Although the loco looks very smart in this BR green livery, it has never actually worn it since conversion to a Class 33/1 back in 1967. Rail blue had then just been chosen to be the new standard livery for BR vehicles. However, one Class 33/1, 33119, did appear in green livery, but it was soon given a coat of blue paint. 11 May 2003.

From the far west of England across to the east now as we arrive at the Spa Valley Railway. The line's operating base is at Tunbridge Wells West, and it is here we see an absolutely immaculate 33063 *RJ Mitchell* coming off the shed to work a train. Although it has only carried its name (the man who designed the famous Spitfire fighter of World War Two) during preservation, the Railfreight Construction livery is totally authentic, being one of a small batch of the class that received it in the late 1980s. 5 August 2006.

Sealion

Above: The other resident member of the class on the line is the highest numbered '33/0', 33065 *Sealion*. The smart BR blue loco is seen at Groombridge, which at this time was the limit of the line from Tunbridge Wells West. 5 August 2006.

Left: Home to 33110 for many years from 1993 was the Bodmin & Wenford Railway, but it was recently sold to a private owner in 2020 and is currently under restoration, believed to be located in Essex. The loco is seen at Bodmin General. Inexplicably, I have lost all the other images I took this day (pre-digital), so this is the sole image remaining of my visit here! Circa 2002.

This is 33065 *Sealion* and 33063 *RJ Mitchell* departing Groombridge with a train for Tunbridge Wells West. Interesting to note the old Southern Railway milepost, more or less a thing of the past on the modern railway. 5 August 2006.

A colourful triple header with 33063 *RJ Mitchell*, 33065 *Sealion* and 20118 *Saltburn-by-the Sea* approaching Pokehill Crossing with a train for Groombridge. The Class 20 was visiting from its base at the time of the South Devon Railway, and has since returned to the main line. 5 August 2006.

For the last part of this section, we head back west and visit the West Somerset Railway. Both 33048 and 33057 are based here, with 33048 seeing the longest time in service. The loco is seen in the bay platform at Bishops Lydeard in the company of Class 25 25173 *John F Kennedy*, which was also resident on the line for around 15 years until moving to pastures new during 2011. 11 May 2002.

For a while, the loco wore BR green livery with full yellow ends, which some locos sported during the transition period from BR green to BR blue in the late 1960s/early 1970s. It is seen arriving at Crowcombe Heathfield with a Minehead to Bishops Lydeard service. 10 June 2011.

Ticking over patiently awaiting departure time at Bishops Lydeard, the loco has charge of a service for Minehead. Note the '62' in the headcode box denoting a Waterloo to Exeter line service in BR days. 25 October 2008.

Framed by the arch of a minor road bridge near Woolston, between Stogumber at Williton, 33048 is approaching with a Minehead to Bishops Lydeard service. 9 May 2004.

With the superb surroundings of the well-maintained station at Crowcombe Heathfield providing the location, 33048 has the signal to depart with a Bishops Lydeard to Minehead train.

By the late 2010s, 33048 had undergone a thorough overhaul and is currently back in BR green carrying its original D6566 number. Surrounded by summer blooms, the loco is seen waiting to depart Blue Anchor with a service for Minehead. 10 June 2018.

Moving on to the line's other member of the class, 33057 was originally to have been a source of spares for 33048, but it was eventually decided to restore the loco in its own right, and it returned to service on the line during 2012. A couple of years after arriving on the line, however, the loco was looking in a sorry state, seen here stored in a siding at Williton in grey primer to try and slow the rust. 15 June 2007.

Almost 11 years to the day, and 33057 is looking somewhat better now! The loco gets into its stride soon after departure from Blue Anchor with a Minehead-bound train. 10 June 2018.

Time for a few double-headers now as 33048 and D1010 *Western Campaigner* prepare to depart Williton with a Minehead service. On this occasion, the Class 52 Western had developed a fault that could not immediately be rectified, so the Class 33 was summoned from Williton Depot to assist the train forward, making for what would have been a very rare pairing in BR days. 16 June 2007.

The pairing of immaculate twins 33057 and 33048 is seen approaching Blue Anchor on a perfect early summer's day with a Minehead to Bishops Lydeard train. The signaller stands ready to receive the token from one of the traincrew. 10 June 2018.

The pair are seen again, this time during the short period both were in service in the early 2010s (just before 33048 was withdrawn for an overhaul) coming around the curve just after passing the level crossing at Roebuck Lane, west of Crowcombe Heathfield. 8 June 2013.

Many excellent diesel galas have also taken place on this line over the years, and during the one held in 2004, 33103 *Swordfish* and 33202 *Meteor*, both then operating on the main line for Fragonset Railways, were amongst some of the guest locos. The two locos are seen at Coombe Florey, a few miles west of Bishops Lydeard, with a train from Minehead to Bishops Lydeard. 8 May 2004.

With the gorse flowers just coming into bloom in the background, the same paring of 33202 *Meteor* and 33103 *Swordfish* are heading around the curve at Roebuck Farm this time, just south of Crowcombe Heathfield, with a Bishops Lydeard to Minehead service. 8 May 2004.

I thought that a fitting conclusion to this book on Class 33s would be this shot of all three sub-classes on one train, and in the right order too! 33048, 33103 *Swordfish* and 33202 *Meteor* are seen approaching Leigh Woods level crossing, soon after leaving Stogumber station, with a Minehead to Bishops Lydeard service. This combination has happened a few times before on various heritage lines, and I believe at least once on the main line, but it is always worth seeing again! 9 May 2004.

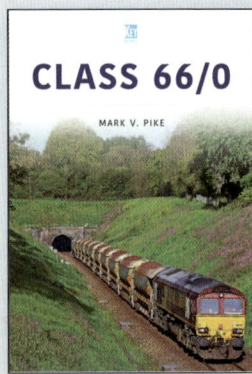
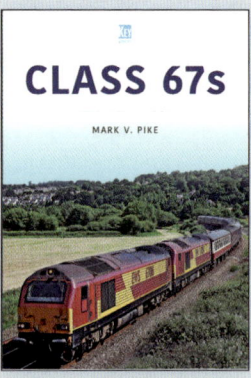
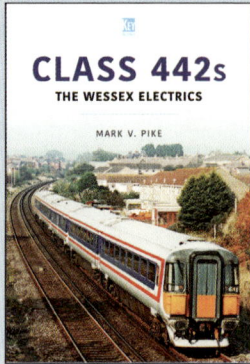

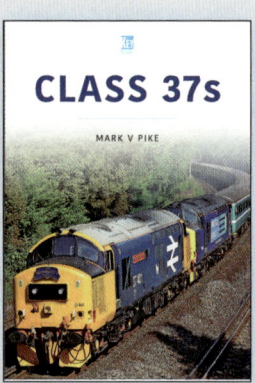
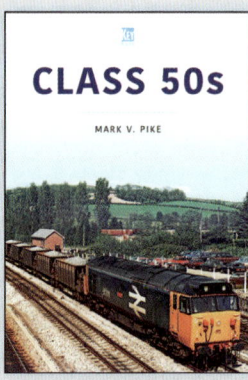